ALPHA

BESSORA   BARROUX

ALPHA

ABIDJAN TO GARE DU NORD

TRANSLATED FROM THE FRENCH BY
SARAH ARDIZZONE

THE
BUCKET
LIST

First published in 2016 in Great Britain by
The Bucket List, 18 Walker Street, Edinburgh, EH3 7LP

Title of the original French edition
"Alpha: Abidjan – Gare du Nord" © 2014 Gallimard

Text © 2014 Gallimard
Illustrations © 2014 Gallimard
Translation © 2016 Sarah Ardizzone

A CIP catalogue record for this book is available from the British
Library upon request

ISBN: 978-1-911370-00-0

Printed in Europe

INSTITUT
FRANÇAIS
ROYAUME-UNI

This book is supported by the Institut français (Royaume-Uni) as part of the Burgess programme

Supported using public funding by
**ARTS COUNCIL
ENGLAND**

*This book has been selected to receive English PEN's PEN Promotes and PEN Translates Awards, supported by Bloomberg
and Arts Council England as part of the Writers in Translation programme. English PEN exists to promote literature and its
understanding, uphold writers' freedoms around the world, campaign against the persecution and imprisonment of writers for
stating their views, and promote the friendly co-operation of writers and free exchange of ideas. www.englishpen.org*

Here is a book we should all be reading, young and old, of whatever country and continent, of whatever religion, or of no religion, of whatever political persuasion or none. Here is a writer and illustrator of formidable talent, who tell a searing tale of our time, the tale of the migrant, the refugee, the unwanted of this world.

It is not a comfortable read for us in the comparative comfort of Western society. No punches are pulled. It is a stark and seemingly hopeless story. But even in this desperate tale the human spirit shines through. There is the fierce determination of the refugee, the asylum seeker, to escape, to endure, never to give up.

Read it and weep. We weep because we know how fortunate we are, because we do so little to reach out and help those who need us most. So often we pass by on the other side. So often we look away. Once you read this deeply troubling book, passing by, looking away, is no longer an option.

MICHAEL MORPURGO

IN MEMORY OF ANNE GORMAND.
THANKS TO TOGOLA.
THANKS TO THE JARDIN D'ALICE.

BARROUX

I imagine Europe is beautiful, but very cold too. There isn't dust like there is in Africa. The roads are in good condition. I'm sure it's cleaner than where I come from. I think Europe is a good place to live.

My sister-in-law has a hair salon in Paris, near the Gare du Nord. That's where they are, I suppose. But they never call me. A phone call from Paris to Abidjan is expensive. And I can't call them. I've run out of credit.

My name is Alpha and I'm a cabinet-maker. My family name is Coulibaly, so it sounds like I might be from Mali. But I'm not from Mali, I'm from Côte d'Ivoire. Marital status – a wife and a child. My wife and son left me behind in Abidjan. They never call me. There's no news.

Patience and Badian set off for Paris. No, they didn't have a visa. I mean, have you ever been to the consulate? The three of us went there to start with.

Application for a short-stay Schengen Visa, which is what someone from Côte d'Ivoire needs to enter France. Purpose of travel – visit to family or friends, tourism. Duration of stay – less than three months. The consulate wanted proof of enrolment at the Commercial Registration Office as validated by the District Court of Abidjan, etc. That's because I'm a tradesman. But we weren't going to France on business – we were going to visit my sister-in-law.

For my wife, they required confirmation of employment, holiday leave, etc. Well. That's impossible. "Furthermore," they said, "furthermore" … persons working as private domestic staff in Côte d'Ivoire must present a letter from their employer, who undertakes not to make the visa applicant work during their stay in France. Why did they ask this? Does my wife look like a cleaner?

They also required – "furthermore" as they put it – proof of sponsorship and/or private accommodation issued by the relevant French authority (faxes not valid). Then more paperwork, for accommodation. "Furthermore," they insisted, "furthermore," the applicant must produce 25 euros per day, excluding accommodation costs, in travellers' cheques or cash in euros (with the exchange receipt). Enough to live like kings. And that's not counting the administration fee. Non-reimbursable in the event the visa is refused. And on top of that – "furthermore" – proof of health insurance, repatriation for medical reasons, travel documentation, a detailed itinerary, etc. Seek advice from your travel agent.

So, when you leave the consulate, one thing's for sure – you understand that Côte d'Ivoire loves France more than France loves Côte d'Ivoire. But, seeing as Côte d'Ivoire doesn't love its own people very much either, Ivorians still flee for Europe. My wife and my son left six months ago, without visas, that's right. I took out a loan to pay for their passage as far as Mali. I don't really know what route they took after that. They wanted to reach the Gare du Nord, and my sister-in-law's hair salon.

My grandfather fought for France in the war. 1939–1945. Perhaps he can help me get to the Gare du Nord, seeing as he was a war hero in France. They gave him medals for surviving his injuries. Back then, he even had French nationality. The colonised became French, that was the law. So my grandfather advises me to show his French nationality papers to the consulate. That way, there'll be no more visa problems.

But guess what? The consulate says no. "What you need to understand," the consulate says, "is that your grandfather didn't become a full French citizen, but rather a common law subject, which isn't the same thing. The fact of the matter is, your grandfather isn't French, and neither are you. I'm sorry, but you can always apply for a short-stay visa. Now for that you would need to present … "Furthermore," as they like to say.

Outside, I climb into a taxi. But it isn't any old taxi. This taxi belongs to Valtis. And Valtis isn't your average taxi-driver-fisherman-barman. Every day, between 3 p.m. and 4 p.m., he waits at the consulate gates. That's when people leave, after waiting since morning for the consulate to make them give up hope. Valtis is there to console them. "What, you didn't get a visa? Well, who can get a visa these days? I even know a diplomat who was refused on the grounds that he was too old and sick to get health insurance. Nobody can get a visa these days. Not even if they're married to a white person."

Within ten minutes, Valtis has made you feel better. He knows people who can open the doors of the world for you. Malians, Mauritanians, Nigerians … there are even Algerians who can drive you all the way to Holland. "Is it a crime to want to help my brothers reach Europe so they can support their relatives who've stayed behind?" Europe costs. But it's worth it at any price.

Take me, Alpha. I have so many plans for my family, so many dreams. The problem is money. I explain to Valtis that I haven't got any. I still owe 12,000 euros for my wife and son's journey. I pay back a little every month, but I'm counting on my wife to send me money from Paris so we can pay it off more quickly. By helping her sister at the hair salon and by looking after children. But I haven't had any news … The only thing for it is to sell my cabinet-making business.

The business isn't worth much because customers are few and far between. But Valtis explains that I can use the shop to clear part of my previous debt, as well as paying for my passage to Gao, in Mali. He shows me the routes on a map. The path you choose dictates where you'll end up. You might stay in a camp in the middle of the desert, or wait by the sea, and you could waste five or six years.

Still, five or six years on the move is better than rotting here. Yes, there's a chance you'll die before you reach your destination, but if you stay here you'll be dead a lot sooner. You never know what the journey has in store for you. But you can be sure about what's waiting for you if you stay – nothing.

I can't afford to end up just anywhere. I have to get to the Gare du Nord. That's why Valtis shows me the maps. It's important to plan my route so I can be sure of getting there. Imagining it is a bit like arriving ahead of time. Valtis can only guarantee my journey as far as Gao, in Mali. After that, I'll need luck on my side.

There are several possible routes. I can travel to Senegal, Mauritania, Morocco, Tunisia, or even Libya. I can aim for the Canary Islands, Malta, Spain, and who knows where else. There are too many towns and camps for me to remember them all.

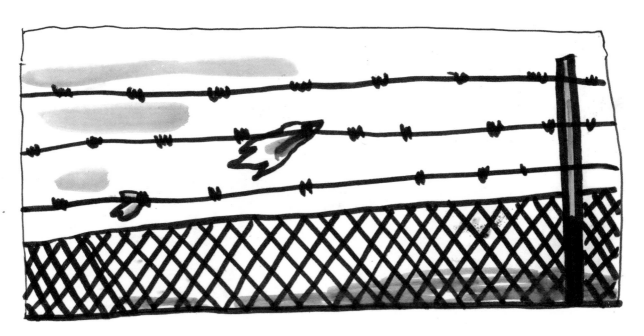

In any case, what I've learned is that the most dangerous routes are also the least risky. So, if you travel by sea from Saint-Louis in Senegal, there's a chance you'll drown, but the police are less likely to catch you. How mad is that? But if you stick to dry land all the way to the 'Little Berlin Wall', there's Spanish barbed wire and border guards to shoot you down. The Little Berlin Wall protects two cities that Spain controls in Morocco – Ceuta and Melilla.

Now don't go thinking the countries in North Africa are any more generous than Europe or Côte d'Ivoire. Europe is so afraid of us that its Mediterranean neighbours keep a sharp eye on their borders, in return for a lot of money. All those countries are bribed with aid money. So who's it supposed to 'aid', this aid money? I don't know, but the result is that North Africa isn't always very welcoming towards its sub-Saharan neighbours.

Selling my cabinet-making business isn't easy. Who's got money in Abidjan to buy a shop? Nobody puts in an offer. Valtis suggests I do a deal with one of the gang bosses. According to Valtis, my cabinet-making business is worth no more than my passage to Gao. I have to hand over the keys to the shop as security. As well as the keys to my house, next door to the shop.

What else can I do? I don't care – I know I'm leaving for ever. They can have my house, I'm leaving tomorrow. If I have to return one day, it'll mean I've died along the way. I take a small suitcase, and a photo of Patience and Badian. I'll show it everywhere I go. Perhaps some of my fellow adventurers will have met them on the road?

On departure day, I'm as happy as I would be at a birth, but I'm also grieving as if somebody had died. That somebody is me. It kills me to abandon my country like this, but I'm being reborn by walking towards a new destiny. Finding my wife and son.

We plan to leave at dawn, but our old Lada Niva refuses to start before the morning's almost over. Next to us, a Renault 4 doesn't want to start either. The European cars here are old. Everybody joins in pushing to start us off and, at last, vroom vroom. Both cars are on their way.

There's a lot of people inside the Lada, and on the roof too, surrounded by luggage spilling over on both sides of the car. I keep my suitcase with me.

The boy sitting next to me is dressed as if he were going to school. He pretended to his parents that he was off to his classes as usual. Right now, his mother thinks he's still there. Eventually, she'll realise that he skipped school today. Perhaps she'll still be waiting for him in ten years' time. There are some people you spend your whole life waiting for.

I start talking to a funny guy called Antoine. He's from Cameroon and he wants to go to Spain, so he can play for F.C. Barcelona. "Ronaldinho, Ronaldo, Yaya Touré ... I want to join them. I want to be better than them." His parents and eight brothers are so confident he'll be signed, and so convinced he'll be paid millions of euros, that they've all clubbed together to pay for his trip. He's powerfully built, this Antoine. He's already wearing his football boots.

A girl is saying that being alive is the only thing that matters. As long as there's life, there's hope. She counts herself lucky because she's alive. She's accompanying a very sick old man. He's going to Europe for treatment because it seems the hospitals in his country don't work. He tells me he's never been on a plane before, just like the rest of us. And he's never left his country before, just like the rest of us. He's been told that he simply has to cross the water and he'll be in Spain. They've lied to him, for sure. There are some truths that are best kept quiet.

It makes me laugh that we're beginning our journey on an avenue called Boulevard de la Paix. Peace Boulevard? Yeah, right. Time passes, and nothing changes. You're young, you're strong and you're motivated. But there's always a wall blocking your way. We're driving along now. The flies are buzzing around us and I'm all fired up. I keep the photo of Patience and Badian close to my heart.

This is it, we're on the open road at last. I'm breathing in great lungfuls of air – nothing can stop me now. Driving like this makes you feel you can change your life. And nobody will stand in your way. Perhaps I'll find Patience in Gao? Or people who'll recognise her from the photo. The Lada driver doesn't want to tell us when we'll get there. He doesn't say much. I think it's because he doesn't know.

There's a problem with the radiator. We spend the night here. Some people sleep in the car, others on the roof, a few lie down by the roadside. I go with the driver to find something to fix the leak. We melt some rubber and bitumen to plug the hole.

We're off again. The driver seems in a bad mood. From what I can see on his dashboard, we've done nearly eight hundred kilometres. Does that mean we're in a different country now? I haven't seen any border guards. If we'd passed a customs checkpoint I'd have noticed, because I didn't sleep at all last night. I never imagined Côte d'Ivoire could be so big. Or that it would take so long to leave it.

The driver has stopped by the roadside. True to his vow of silence, he refuses to talk. The silence is creepy. Why have we suddenly pulled over, when we were driving along just fine? Will it be the police next? I'm not breathing as calmly as I was a while back. Everybody in the car is waiting for the driver to say something. But he says nothing.

The hours go by. The driver just stares at his watch. At 10 p.m. he starts up again. Five minutes later, I can see the border. Zégoua. Why did the driver make us wait for four hours, three kilometres from the border with Mali? Two armed men let us pass, in return for an envelope that's handed to them by the driver.

So we're in Mali. Not that it makes much difference. In the pitch black, all you can see is the road in the headlight. I say 'headlight' because only one of them is working. And it only works on full beam.

The driver keeps going through the night. I doze. I drift in and out of a bad dream, where I can see Patience and Badian's faces. Did they take the same route as me? Did they travel in a Lada Niva? Are they hungry? My stomach's grumbling, but I'm too tense to eat. I suck on some sugar cane. After that, I feel a bit better.

When I wake up, I check the sun. It's very high in the sky, so I guess it's midday. We're driving along Avenue de l'Unité Africaine. The idea of African Unity makes me laugh – African Unity! We drive, we drive, we drive, and Antoine sings the Spanish national anthem. It's his way of getting ready to join Barcelona.

The schoolboy is still staring out of the window. Sometimes he turns towards the driver and taps him on the shoulder to ask where the desert is. The Sahara. The name seems to frighten him. Me too, it frightens me. But it makes me dream as well. The calmest person is the old man seeking treatment in Europe. His son works as a nurse in the cancer ward of an Italian hospital. But this sick old man still couldn't get a visa.

His request for medical evacuation never reached the offices of the Italian consulate in Congo – it got stuck with the Congolese state services. He asked for a medical evacuation but he didn't get an answer, the MPs were on recess. I'm thirsty. There's nothing left to drink. Because of the delay, because of the radiator breaking down, because of the litres of water we couldn't transport, because of the litres we wasted, and because you always think you can get by on the minimum. I'm thirsty. I'm drinking the red dust of this soil – the more it enters my nose, the thirstier I feel. What'll it be like in the desert?

Bamako. The capital of Mali. Some of our company are taking a different route, for Senegal. The old man and his daughter leave us here. I don't know if they understand the risks involved. I don't know if they've looked at a map, like I have.

Because when it comes to catching a smuggler's boat from Saint-Louis to the Canaries, even the official shipping lines are deadly. Didn't the capsizing of the *Joola* cause more deaths than the *Titanic*? As for one of those worn-out rubber dinghies that set out in bad weather for the Spanish islands ... I don't want to become a 'boat person'. There are rumours that the dinghies are so overloaded they start sinking before they even get out to sea.

The group splits in two. I'm with those who are carrying on to Gao. We're a long way from leaving Mali. And if we do manage to leave, I couldn't say exactly what country we'd be entering.

All I want is to keep my feet on dry land for as long as possible. Perhaps all the way to the barbed wire of the Little Berlin Wall, in the north of Morocco.

The driver takes us to a small wooden chapel, near the caves of Bamako, in the hillside of Koulouba, at the end of Route de la Liberté. Tucked away, this secret chapel is maintained by and for adventurers like us.

Our thirst is quenched and our bellies filled, thanks to a Cameroonian who's staying at the chapel. He serves us food and drink. Eugène explains that he helps look after the place, a church for those in transit, where several adventurers take it in turns to give the sermon. They sing together, as one. It restores the travellers' strength.

Eugène isn't just a caretaker. He's an unemployed sociologist. "I can remember the exact day I left. I walked out of the house on a Wednesday. It'll be five years ago on 1st October. 'Have a good day,' my father said to me. I can still picture him as if it were yesterday. He was wearing a blue shirt." The schools in Eugène's country don't want to recruit him as a teacher, because he has 'opinions'. It seems the government only recruits signed-up members of the ruling party.

As for the private schools, they bring over European expats who don't meddle in politics. Eugène wanted to become an expat too. Apparently, it's more complicated in the opposite direction. Eugène hasn't given up on his hopes of becoming a teacher. In the meantime, he cleans the chapel, and he also does the odd bit of building work for people. For him, it was a case of leaving or dying – "It felt like there was boiling water inside my head. To cool it down, I had to leave …"

I arrive in Gao ten days later. The Lada driver unloads his cargo and sets off again in the direction of Guinea, I think, to pick up a new batch of adventurers. That's what I heard him saying on the phone.

Gao is bristling with touts. All vying to win you over. With their toothpaste smiles, they boast about the advantages of going with them. But examine their mouths more closely and you'll see how rotten they are. When you're relying on someone, you don't want to know he's got rotten teeth.

You're seduced by the nice photos of the Eiffel Tower they dangle from their hands. "With us, you're sure to arrive at the right port!" they promise. But which port? No one ever knows. "Your life is in my hands!" Who do they think they are? God? The thing is, they have as much power as God.

Anyway, I don't have any more money. So I'm staying here for a while to save up again, find a good smuggler, pay him, on credit if possible, or in exchange for a future favour. Did Patience and Badian come this way?

Antoine and I have found a small job in a cement works, cash in hand. Every morning, we put on our overalls. It's back-breaking work. And it doesn't pay much.

I meet adventurers in Gao whose nerves and resources are so strained that they don't even know which country they're in any more. Some of them think they're already in southern Algeria. Others imagine they're in Mauritania. That's what the desert does to you.

I can't afford to make mistakes. I need to know precisely where I am. I'm in Mali. And I always need to know exactly where I'm going. I'm going to the Gare du Nord. My biggest challenge is to follow the same route as my wife and son, when they probably just took the first opportunity that came their way.

They say that Mauritania is cheaper, but Morocco is a safer bet, even if the Spanish enclaves have become impassable. It doesn't matter, there's always a way.

Even if it means travelling 2,000 kilometres in the wrong direction to catch a dugout canoe at Nouadhibou, I'll be back. And when I say 2,000, perhaps it's a bit more than that? Still, I won't let a thousand kilometres get in my way.

I hope Patience and Badian went via Morocco. But I can't find anyone in Gao who remembers them. It's not surprising – the population here changes all the time, camps go up and come down and go up again. Some form small towns that last for a while.

These towns are made to be deserted, to return to dust, without leaving any traces or memories behind. Ghost towns. Except in the minds of those who lived in them.

I've been waiting in Gao for months now. This journey's so tough. You see tourists in Abidjan, Bamako and Gao. Americans, French, happy people touring around Africa on bicycles.

Did anyone ask them for proof of enrolment at the Commercial Registration Office as validated by the District Court of Paris, a 'taxpayer's account number', an import licence, bank account or post office statements, proof of address, and their most recent receipts proving commercial purchases made in Côte d'Ivoire or Mali?

Because they ask us for that. They erect barriers, bang, bang, bang, barbed wire at Ceuta and Melilla, bang, bang, bang, sniffer dogs trained to find illegal migrants, sniff, sniff, sniff, and watchtowers. We can't just go touring wherever we want. So we look for work to pay our way by car, by boat or on foot. It's five times more expensive than a plane ticket. I'm tired. I'm going crazy. But as long as I'm not dead, I'll get out of Mali in the end.

Finding work isn't easy. All the jobs are already taken, and because the adventurers passing through Gao don't have any papers, they're badly paid. So badly paid it takes them years to buy a passage to Morocco, or to the Mauritanian coast.

My surname – Coulibaly – is common in Mali. But I don't speak Bambara, so I can't pass myself off as local. I'm just another 'illegal' migrant here. But I'm not a criminal. And I work hard. Antoine and I have found a new job, to supplement the one at the cement works – it's in a rubbish dump.

I've discovered that Coulibaly means 'without a dugout' … So perhaps I should travel via Morocco rather than Mauritania. When you're without a dugout you're better off not travelling by water! I'm going crazy I tell you … I'm desperate for money. To make money in Gao, you either get ripped off by rich Malians or you start dealing, especially in drugs.

During the five months I've spent in Gao, I've been a labourer at the cement works, a rubbish collector, and a shop assistant for a cloth merchant who kept putting off payday until tomorrow. Eventually I understood he was waiting for his customers to pay him, and that they kept putting off paying their bills until tomorrow … When I left Abidjan, I never imagined it would be so difficult. Part of me suspected it might be. But the other part of me didn't want to believe it. That other part is the glimmer of hope that keeps me going.

New arrivals every day, from Guinea, Nigeria, Cameroon ... From all sorts of places – Africa is so huge. They need protection, and promises.

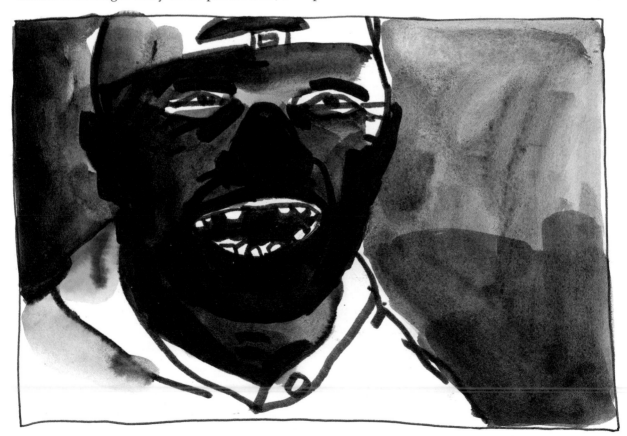

Because you can't move around here for people on the make – con-artists claiming they'll get you as far as Morocco. It almost comes as a relief to put your money in their pockets, in a bid to convince yourself a bit more. "Till tomorrow," they say, "same time, same place!" But the next day, no one.

Sometimes they sell you fake passports that are so bad it's funny. It's hard to tell who's honest and who's not. At the end of the day, the best way to earn some cash is by smuggling.

So my new job is as a people-smuggler. I've decided to do what the bandits do, but honestly. I sell journeys, except I offer 50% credit, and I don't vanish into thin air the next day.

I'm planning our route. Time drags on. Some adventurers have been waiting a fortnight. Others four years. Shopkeepers, fishermen and even former civil servants have left everything behind them for an illusion – shimmering like a mirage in the desert.

I've been stagnating in Gao for eight months. I've made a lot of promises I still can't deliver on – eight adventurers have paid me to help them get as far as Kidal, just before the Algerian border.

I make sure I'm paid in euros. Dollars are good too. More and more adventurers are trying their luck in Canada. Some are aiming for China. Others are headed for the southern African countries, or stopping north of the Sahara.

And the Europeans think they're taking on all the misery in the world. If Patience's sister wasn't close to the Gare du Nord, I'd have preferred Australia. The thing is, we don't choose where we're born, or where we migrate to. We make do, we go where we can.

With my euros, I'm looking to rent a car. Because I've given credit to some of the adventurers waiting for their passage, I don't have much cash. Plus I've built up debts. My passengers probably won't be able to pay me the rest of what they owe. But perhaps I'll find someone who can lend me a car to get to Kidal without too much cash up front?

Half cash, half on credit. Or in exchange for who knows what. It's an economy of favours.

Abebi is from Lagos. She's been living in Gao for two years. And, in the space of those two years, she tells me that she met Patience and Badian. She recognised them straight away when I showed her the photo. But she won't tell me any more. The price of her story is the trip.

She'll only talk if I drive her and the others as far as Kidal. Abebi will be my ninth passenger. I can feel some hope returning. Still, when you think that on an Airbus, it only takes six hours and 1,500 euros to reach Paris.

Of course, I didn't find an Airbus. But I'm not unhappy with the minibus that an old fisherman has sold me. He was so ancient he didn't want to rent it to me, because he said he'd be dead soon. So I bought it for the price of a cheap rental.

The bus is nearly as old as its owner. The ignition's gone, but you can start it up by jiggling the wires. It's a German make. Germans are the best when it comes to cars.

Fresh supplies. We pile our belongings onto the roof – bags, water cans, sleeping bags, mattresses, cooking pots, provisions. And even two bicycles. Again, everything's spilling over on all sides. Abebi is sick, she keeps vomiting. But we can't delay our departure.

Everyone is set on leaving right away. Especially Abebi. She hasn't had much luck. Women don't have much choice when it comes to making money to pay for their passage.

Either they take care of the children, or they take care of the husbands. Abebi chose the husbands. It was better paid. She's worked so hard she's wrecked. Everybody in Gao looks down on her. Especially the husbands who used her services. Yes, it's time to leave.

I'm good at fixing things, so I'll make the Volkswagen last as far as Kidal. The desert is spread out before us. We've only got 350 kilometres to cover.

A little boy arrives just as we're about to leave. Or rather, he's brought to us by force. He's putting up a fight like a child possessed. He's six or seven and skinny as a rake. He says he wants to stay in Gao. And find his mother again. The girl accompanying him cries until there are no tears left.

She might be thirteen or fourteen. She holds out an envelope stuffed with notes and begs me to take her little brother. Their mother, a Senegalese market trader, has just been arrested by the police. The big sister tells me there's plenty of money in the envelope. Much more than the cost of the passage to Spain. She'll give me the whole lot, if I promise to take good care of her brother. His name is Augustin. And she's Augusta, but she has to stay here. To try and get her mother out of prison.

But the child refuses to let go of his sister's hand. This lasts an hour perhaps, an hour of tears and begging. In the end, I give half the money back to Augusta. She's going to need it here. And I get the little boy into the bus by force. I make up a terrible lie to sweeten the pill. Yes, of course his mother's going to join us along the way, perhaps at the next stopping point.

Almost reassured, Augustin sticks a finger in his mouth and closes his eyes. So there are ten of us, in the final count. All aboard. Off we go. Some of the passengers even sing.

The Volkswagen might have German nationality, but it worries me more than a Russian plane. Smoke pours from the engine every now and then.

And then it stops. The minibus holds out. But we've still got the problem of water. And the barricades.

We make it through the barricades using 'tranquillisers', the small sums of money we give the soldiers to help relax their finger on the trigger. Without these, they shoot adventurers like rabbits. Who would lodge a complaint? Nobody's going to claim your corpse.

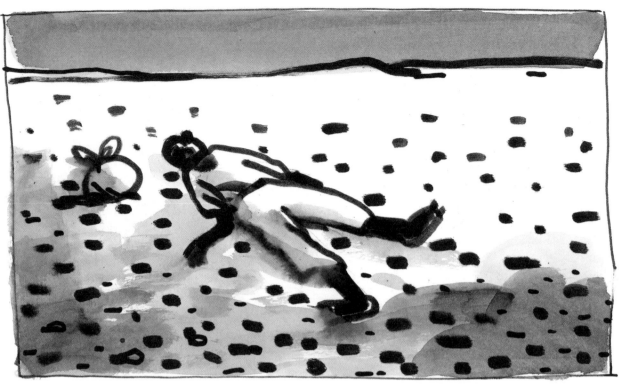

Not even your own mother would know you'd got bullet holes through your chest somewhere in the Sahara. The point is, soldiers never accept anything on credit. And if you haven't got any 'tranquillisers', they won't hold back on the bullets.

We have to go around the next barricade. I'm inexperienced at this and they spot us.

I can hear the bullets whistling through the air. They're firing at us. But the bullets don't even graze us. These soldiers are known for their alcoholism. They've got their own problems.

By way of detour after detour, we head closer to Kidal. Very quickly, I learn to avoid the barricades.

We stop a lot. Abebi is vomiting froth. She has no bile left. She's spitting bubbles of saliva. We've been on the road for nine hours, and we still haven't covered two hundred kilometres.

Darkness falls. Perhaps Abebi will feel better tomorrow. Augustin sucks his fingers in silence.

It's a cold night. We sleep huddled together, forming a sort of human radiator. We can't even make a fire – the smoke would betray us.

Augustin snuggles against me. My lie has restored his trust. It breaks my heart. The sound of his breathing reminds me of my son. And so does his smell. Augustin tells me he misses his sister, and his mother. But he's glad he'll be seeing them soon.

The next morning, before dawn, I spot Antoine jogging. He's maintaining his form, he says, so he can sign with Barcelona.

We've run out of water. This is such a wretched discovery that everyone starts to laugh hysterically. What else can we do? "I'm prepared to drink urine," Antoine says, "but only my own!"

Abebi isn't feeling any better. Or any worse, for that matter. She asks to be left on the sand, so the desert can bury her alive. That way, at least, she'll have a grave. I sense that some of our company would abandon Abebi to her fate.

We all leave together.

Kidal looms into view after another eight hours of driving. Algeria isn't very far now.

The engine of the Volkswagen gives up the ghost at the gates of Kidal. The old German minibus didn't want to cross the border ... it liked Mali better! Buses are like people really – they might have wheels, but they're not keen on being displaced.

The minibus is dead, but there's still plenty to be done with it.

I'm going to strip it clean. Three rear-view mirrors, two tyres (four in total, but two of them are too far gone). One steering wheel, the seats and headrests. There's the battery as well – we should get something for it. And what else? The cylinder head, and some scrap metal.

There's nothing left to pick off the carcass. It'll provide shelter for the grasses and shade for the scorpions.

Kidal is a devout town. Our arrival has restored some colour to Abebi. But not to Augustin. The little boy was hoping to find his mother. How much longer will he believe my lie? I can't tell him that his mother is more likely to die in prison than to be reunited with him on the road.

We have to stay in a camp. There are two of them.

Those who can work as builders, as cooks, as painter-decorators, tailors or mobile phone repairers are put up in the cleaner one. For everyone else …

… meaning us, we're lumped in with the beggars. Still, with everything we salvaged from the minibus, we should've been able to set ourselves up as scrap metal dealers, or spare parts sellers. But it turns out all the beggars are some kind of scrap metal dealers.

The good news is we've managed to stay together. Normally there's the Malian section, the Guinean section, and so on. We're living with the Senegalese, where we've each taken over a section of a room. Antoine has hung up the Spanish flag on the wall in his corner.

We nail two or three planks of wood to the wall so we can put away our shoes and save space. On the floor, there's only room for the mattress and a crate that doubles as a table. The mattress is older than I am. It's seen a lot of bodies come and go. It smells. Of urine.

How long are we going to stay here? It's dirty. Washing is hung out to dry on lines strung up between the huts.

But you can't wash away the dust. And it's not just in the streets – the dust has settled in people's hearts. The Congolese rumba blares out, but no one's dancing. Augustin looks moody. Has he unravelled my lie?

How many months will it take to find a new route? New smugglers? Money? Abebi wants to start working again, even though she doesn't think she'll find many clients in Kidal. Except perhaps among the foreign visitors in the camp opposite …

Anyway, she's been cleaning. In one corner of the room, she's put out her toiletries on the floor, to show she's hygienic and not infected. But there's nothing she can do about the mattress – it still stinks.

Tarik is an Algerian people-smuggler. His pick-up truck is even more dilapidated than my minibus was, but he's clear-headed. There are two possible routes heading out of Kidal – through southern Algeria, as far as Tin Zaouatine, or you can enter Algeria via the north of Mali. According to Tarik, the easiest way is with a Malian passport. Malians don't need a visa to enter Algeria.

Then after Tin Zaouatine … Well, since we don't want to travel by sea, the Algerian and Moroccan networks will get us to the Little Berlin Wall. They say you don't decide the route – it's the route that decides for you.

The only thing we're sure about – Abebi, Augustin, Antoine and me – is that we want to stay together for as long as possible. I explain this to Tarik. I also show him a photo of my family, so he understands why I have to reach the Gare du Nord. Paris. France. Not just any old place, like those people who've ended up somewhere in Europe and don't know how they've got there. Tarik's never seen my wife and my son. He'll ask his colleagues.

Two weeks after our arrival in Kidal, I've found out a lot. Tarik smuggles petrol and cigarettes between Mali and Algeria. I understand. You get by as best you can. He sells drugs too, but his partner in crime was killed recently by arms-traffickers.

From what I've understood, Tarik owes a fair bit of money to these traffickers. He's looking for a way out. That's why he's offering to drive us – he's using us as a cover. And that means we can negotiate him down on the price. Abebi isn't so keen. What if the traffickers find Tarik, and us with him?

But Tarik says he's had some information about my family. According to him, they crossed over into southern Algeria, and are still around Tin Zaouatine. There's no time to waste. Even if Abebi doesn't agree, we can't refuse an offer of 200 euros per person instead of 400, with three quarters on credit. If possible, I want to avoid spending any of Augustin's money. He's going to need it.

Everyone's on board. We're off.

The dust fills your nose and mouth. Everyone has their water flask on their knees. Abebi is sulking. She claims that Tarik's a liar. But is she any better? She still hasn't told me what she knows about my family. Even though she'd promised to tell me everything when we reached Kidal.

There's nothing I can do about it. Abebi won't talk, she doesn't trust anyone and she's terrified of me deserting her mid-route. Her silence is her travel insurance. No, her life insurance.

And then she blurts out, "Tarik lied to you! He never saw your wife and son!" Tarik always has beads of sweat on his forehead, whether from the heat or from fear I don't know. He changes his SIM card every day. And we overhear garbled snatches of conversation. Is he speaking in code? He must be picking up news about the route.

And learning about the patrols. Judging by how awful he looks after those phone calls, the news can't be good.

The journey is chaotic. You're going straight ahead. And then suddenly you change direction. A detour. Followed by another. And another.

There's nobody to explain what's going on. And nobody who dares ask – animals prefer not to know when they're being led to the slaughter. It's always like this. And no, you don't get used to it. You just resign yourself to it. That's all.

Tarik committed to driving us as far as the Moroccan border. But before we even reach Tin Zaouatine, he dumps us in the desert.

He says we've got to pay him back the credit we owe. Is that his true reason? It's not what we agreed. But he's the boss here. And when he tips us out, we're less than five hundred metres from the border, on the fringes of a new camp.

I'll never forget the look in Augustin's eyes. I think he's understood I'm not in control of anything. He's understood we're not free. Six years old is on the young side to stop dreaming. In front of us, the camp is vast. Like a town of baked clay huts, with clearly marked-out districts. Two hundred dinars in arrival fees. It's even got its own internal regulations.

There's the Côte d'Ivoire ghetto, the Nigerian ghetto, the Cameroonian ghetto. This time, there's no escape. It's impossible for us all to stay together. Abebi leaves for the Nigerian ghetto, Antoine for the Cameroonian ghetto. I keep Augustin with me in the Côte d'Ivoire ghetto. Nobody knows that he's Senegalese. There are times when Augustin seems so far away. Times when he isn't with us, but with his mother and his sister.

We have a president. Each ghetto has one, together with a vice-president,
a secretary, a treasurer and a security official.

There are those who've been living here for a year or more. Like this law student from
Côte d'Ivoire, who's gone crazy. The state hadn't paid his scholarship grant for seventeen
months, so he left. "A fish has more freedom than I do," he rants all day long. "It can get
to Spain however it fancies … If a fish can get to Spain, then so can I! No way am I going
back to Togo!" He's even forgotten that he comes from Côte d'Ivoire.

And what about Patience? Tarik had assured me she was in Tin Zaouatine. Could she have been in this camp instead? She might be living a few metres away from me.

We look for work to pay for the next stage of the journey. It won't be with Tarik. But we're going to have to pay to get into Algeria. And I'm still looking for Patience and Badian. Nothing. Nobody recognises them from the photo. I can't give up hope. It's only a matter of time. And time is the one thing I do have. I know it's going to take a long time.

Augustin kills time by playing cards with the other children. They play for money. Dollars, African francs, euros and dinars. I don't dare imagine what Abebi's getting up to in her ghetto. I don't know if I'll ever see her again. And what about Antoine?

If you want to eat, you beg at the border. If you're lucky, Algerian families will bring you some goat. But not water. The water we steal from further away.

There's no healthcare. If you have a hernia, tough. The best you can hope for is a rash. Everybody scratches here, and not just their heads. They say it's heat rash. Scabies. Lice. Crabs.

Still no sign of Patience and Badian.

Every day, at around 6 p.m., it's the same old performance. On the Algerian side, we see the trucks pulling up. Hundreds of Africans clamber out, escorted by the security forces. The new deportees arrive in the ghettos, they get divided up, settled in. They're already swearing they'll be off again. "In the name of God, I'm going back to Algeria! Even if it means dying for it." Ker-ching! Two hundred dinars arrival fee. Sign here. Oath of allegiance to your ghetto president.

One evening, we watch a man from Chad arrive, his head swollen from the soldiers' blows. In the absence of a Chad ghetto, the guy becomes Ivorian. The next day, he's dead from his injuries. Burial. Each ghetto has its own cemetery. The graves are to the east of the camp. Facing the rising sun.

The cemetery makes some people want to call home. I listen to a boy leaving a message. "This is the number you can reach me on until tomorrow. If you call me and I don't answer, then either I've made it across, or I'm dead. In that case, I'll try to let you know."

In that case … In this case … In any case, we can have a drink at *L'espoir de Guinée*. A Senegalese man opened this café. There are even strip-lights at the entrance. It means 'The Hope of Guinea', but the guy who opened it doesn't have any hope in anything any more. You'd think he was there to discourage you. "Hey Antoine! That famous dream of yours … F.C. Barcelona. Are you still hoping to get signed?" "You bet!" says Antoine. "More than ever! What doesn't kill me makes me stronger."

We've been stuck in this camp for two months, with no news of the family. Once, when I was fetching water, I ran into Abebi. She's making herself a tidy sum in the Nigerian ghetto. The vice-president of her district protects her in return for his commission. Plus, he helps himself for free. Abebi has traces of scars on her shoulders.

Abebi has lost her faith in everything. "When you know your best clients are in the Algerian security forces, it opens your eyes." She's lost her faith in everything, except the journey. Abebi will soon have enough to pay her passage to the other side, even as far as Spain. She's ready to help out the rest of us a little, seeing as we can't earn half what she does. Antoine and I organise bets on football matches. Each ghetto has its own team, and the Cameroonians are always the hot favourites.

Disappeared. Augustin has disappeared. The little boy vanished from the hut, in the middle of the night. Along with his money. I didn't see or feel or hear anything. Panic. They say there are people who traffic children. Have they taken him?

I pray to all the gods that nobody's taken him. I'd rather believe he went of his own accord. But without telling me? Wouldn't he have told me? All on his own, he has no chance in the desert. I let Abebi and Antoine know.

Antoine is speechless. He can barely swallow. Abebi shrugs. "You win some, you lose some," she says. "Especially when it comes to children." And she heads off to be alone with her grief.

I spend the whole day – and the evening too – scouring the camp, but nobody's seen him. I head back and go to sleep with a bitter taste in my mouth. I can't believe there hasn't been a single sighting. The person who harmed him might be the neighbour who smiles at you in the morning. Where can he have run off to?

In a few months, we should be able to pay a new Tarik. And buy ourselves Malian passports during the 'departure operations'. Everything's for sale. They arrive in big black bags. Real ones stolen from the living or the dead, and fake ones cobbled together with varying degrees of success.

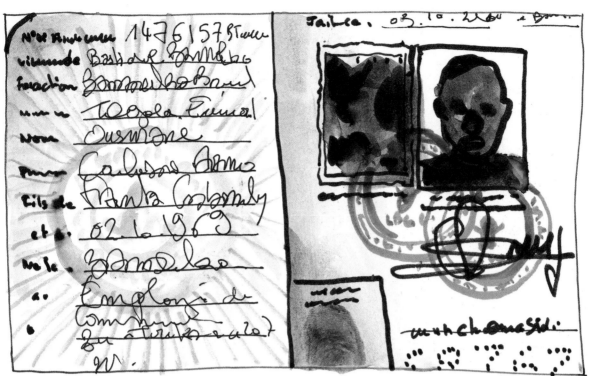

So here we are, kitted out and ready to leave. The photos on our fake passports aren't much of a likeness, but we're told the Algerians won't be able to tell the difference. All black people look the same to them. Who knows? I just wonder whether the guy whose passport I have is still alive.

We wash, we shave, we cut our nails and put on clean clothes, like proper business travellers. One of Tarik's colleagues charges us 2,000 dinars a head to get us across the border. After that, it's anyone's guess. The car's a Peugeot 505, and it's in good condition. We look like regular travellers. It hasn't quite sunk in that we're going to be going through customs. A real customs post, fake passports and four passengers. All aboard. Off we go. Vroom.

The Algerian border. Get out of the car, please. One at a time. The dogs sniff you. Abebi's fine. Antoine's fine. He's sweating, though. Alpha … even I make it through. Still, I sense that they're trying to trip us up. Antoine's sweating profusely now. Only Abebi stays calm … Too calm to have nothing to hide. They're going to grill us. The customs officers question Antoine. In a language I don't understand.

They're speaking to him in Bambara to check he really is Malian. What on earth's come over him? He's saying something in gibberish. And now they're asking him something else? Antoine gives them an answer. The customs officers move to one side with our passports for a few minutes. Five minutes that last an eternity. Then they're back. They're letting us through. I can't believe it. Algeria, I love you! Hey, Antoine, where did you learn to speak Bambara, you crazy Cameroonian? It's thanks to his love life. A while back, Antoine was seeing a Malian girl, with a huge heart and an arse to match!

So this is Algeria. Tomorrow, Morocco. Tarik's associate drops us off at a car wash, which is the place fresh vehicles set off from. Oujda will mark the end of my struggle.

Where are my wife and son? No time to look for them now. We're off again, right away. In a pick-up with three new adventurers on board. They sit in the back and wrap their heads, turban-style, so as not to swallow too much dust. It's third class in the back. But it's still expensive.

I dream of being reunited with my wife and son, in Ceuta or Melilla, in Spain. It makes me cry. Abebi dries my tears. "Don't worry, they weren't in Tin Zaouatine. Tarik lied to you." What about her, why doesn't she say anything? I've mostly given up worrying about how long this is all taking. But today I realise that my journey has lasted more than a year. It's hard to believe. And what about Augustin … Where is Augustin? I'd rather smile. Smiling means surviving.

Abebi doesn't know how to smile, and she won't survive long. She's not at all well. She's tired, sick, worn out, and she's starting to lose her mind. She keeps claiming she's caught 'that disease', AIDS. How can she tell? She's never had a blood test.

I don't know how long we've been driving. It feels like a long time. The driver's navigating with a GPS. I never imagined Africa could be so vast. People always say 'Africa', as if it was a tiny country. They've got no idea.

Let them cross some of Africa on foot, or even in a 4x4, instead of by plane. It's never-ending, it changes all the time, and when you're not closing your eyes to protect them from the dust, you're feeling dizzy from the countryside as it unfolds. So let anyone who pictures Africa as one tiny country travel on foot from the south to the north. I haven't even done half that journey, but I'm telling you the distance will shut them up.

Abebi's eyes become blanker each day. Her journey is a dark night. It's true that we never know where we are. Or where exactly we're being taken. You don't even know if it's dangerous. Or to what degree.

I've done my sums. Thirty days since Tin Zaouatine, two thousand kilometres, four cars, one taxi. They're saying that Morocco is only two days' walk away now. So you walk, you walk, you walk, you're thirsty, your shoulders ache, your legs ache, your back aches, you ache all over.

But you've got callused feet because, as a child, you ran barefoot through the streets of Abidjan, so your heels and toes and the soles of your feet don't hurt. Your feet become your head. Your body obeys them. And you walk, walk, walk, walk.

Oujda in Morocco. Hallelujah. Paradise is only 150 kilometres away, over there, the first Little Berlin Wall – Melilla. We have to wait. For the right moment, and the right smuggler who'll take us on credit. I don't have a cent left, and Abebi's savings have been swallowed up over the last thousand or so kilometres.

Abebi won't be going back to work in her state. We need a doctor. She's emaciated. Someone recommends that we go to see Zaccharia, a Moroccan student.

Zaccharia is studying medicine. He's set up a charity to help 'illegal' migrants. Illegal migrants ... Illegal? What does that even mean? For me, we're adventurers. Indiana Jones would have died eight times over if he'd had to endure what we experience every day. But seeing as Zaccharia can access free treatment for Abebi in a health centre, then yes, fine, I'm happy to be an 'illegal' migrant.

I drift off to sleep in the charity's clean sheets, with the crazy idea that this is paradise. If I wasn't trying to join my wife and son, then yes, Oujda is where I'd stay. And I'd track down Augustin, who'd have walked, and walked, and walked all the way here, on his callused feet.

The doctor has given his verdict. Abebi wasn't wrong. She does have 'that disease'. And the news really isn't good. Because Abebi doesn't just have 'that disease'. She's also pregnant.

On the advice of a Ghanaian woman, Abebi swallows a mixture of leaves. But this fails to cause an abortion. Her belly grows, she doesn't want the child. What would she do with it? One more condemned soul on earth?

Some of the people being looked after by the charity say that pregnant women can travel to Spain, in exchange for the child. But Abebi has given up now. For her, the voyage is over. Abebi will have to stay in Oujda. Antoine and I will stay by her side, for the time being.

The time it takes us to find the money, a smuggler and perhaps some news of Patience and Badian. The charity gives us accommodation, and in the daytime Abebi begs in the courtyard of the university.

Every day, more bad news. This time, from the mouth of a Nigerian man who's just arrived. A small boat bound for Spain split in two this morning. Forty passengers on board, nineteen survivors. The Moroccan coastguards rescued them and drove them to a camp to await deportation. The Nigerian escaped. "You can't look death in the face and throw yourself into her arms."

Four months already. No trace of my family. And no smuggler to take us to Melilla. Everyone keeps talking about how impossible it is to get inside the enclave. Because of the dogs. Because of the barbed wire. Because of the armed police. The gates of paradise are closed again. There's one other possibility – Ceuta. But it's five hundred kilometres from here. And if I can't find a car, am I prepared to walk again?

One morning, Zaccharia rushes to alert me. A student has found Abebi unconscious in the courtyard of the university. There was blood between her legs – she seems to be going into labour earlier than expected. And it hasn't got off to a good start.

I hold her hand. She's losing a lot of blood. And a lot of tears too. She tells me it's her first child. But she's already been pregnant at least five times. The doctor tells her not to talk. But she does. She asks for my forgiveness. Why? Because.

She never knew the whereabouts of my family. She lied. Just like Tarik. To secure her journey. Now she's saying that she won't continue the journey with us. So what's the point of lying any more? The baby doesn't want to come out. Abebi keeps on talking. "Alpha, if the only way is by sea, give up …"

The child is born. It doesn't cry. It's a little girl. And she's dead. Abebi never regains consciousness. I don't know why, but I think of my mother.

I go to collect Abebi's belongings from the university courtyard. A bowl, a few coins and her wrap, which is stained with blood.

There's just Antoine left. "After everything my parents paid to give me a chance with Barcelona, I can't go home empty-handed." We're not giving up. We'll stick together. We have to. Zaccharia gives us a recap on the situation. Melilla is impossible. And there's even less of a chance with Ceuta. Under pressure from Europe, the countries in North Africa have grown hard. The borders between Europe and Africa are controlled twice over. There's only one option left – the boat.

I don't want to. With all these stories of people drowning. My name means without-a-dugout, and I'm thinking of getting in a boat! I mustn't. I can just about swim, but really, I'm without-a-dugout, and I don't want to do it.

Zaccharia puts us in touch with a 'maritime travel agency' – yet more people-smugglers. We climb into a covered truck, full of men and goods. We drive towards the sea. Boat people. I keep Abebi's green and orange wrap close to me.

"The bodies of five illegal migrants of sub-Saharan origin were found on Tuesday on Foum El-Oued beach, near Laayoune, bringing the total number drowned in the area since Monday to twenty-six."

Laayoune. This is where they let us out, in front of a grocery store kept by a Malian who's in transit through Morocco. *Épicerie Las Palmas*. Spain is right opposite. As in the Canary Islands.

But the grocer won't even take us as far as the Canaries.

"Listen up, Coulibaly," the grocer says. "The Atlantic isn't some river or backwater. It's the ocean! Waves that can rise a hundred metres high! Wind that can blow at two hundred kilometres an hour! Is that what you want to face, Antoine? Think about death! You can't talk about life without talking about death. If you climb into a dugout, death will be sitting right next to you."

"Never," says Antoine, who refuses to be discouraged. "It doesn't exist. Not even in my heart."

Antoine says "it" so as not to name her. The one who sits next to you in the dugout. Perhaps it's best not to say her name.

"Are you sure death won't come to you?" the grocer says. "Do you know on which day you were born, Antoine?"

"I know the month, but otherwise I couldn't tell you exactly."

"What about you, Coulibaly?"

"I was born on the 28th of March. In 1900 and something ..."

"Can you tell me on which day you will die?" the grocer asks us.

"I can't even wish for death," says Antoine.

He has said the word. Now will she come?

"Can you tell me where you'll die?"

"Never."

"Can you tell me how you'll die?"

"Never. I know there is something called death, but ..."

"Your future is just dreams," the grocer says. "Tomorrow, go and see the men preparing the fish on the beach. They make two piles. The fresh fish goes to Europe. The rotten fish goes to Nigeria. There you have it, my friend, we're rotten, we're not worth anything to anyone. And you still want to play with the ocean?"

There's nothing for it but to wait.

Nothing for it but to wait until the ocean turns ugly.

When the waves are high and the sea is churned up, the Spanish and Moroccan patrols are less efficient.

The occasional helicopter circles just above the ocean. Like a vulture hovering over its prey. I don't know if it's Spanish or Moroccan, but it's looking for boat people.

Children run on the beach. Where are their parents?

The conditions are right for us to depart. Half a dozen dugouts of every size have been tied up by the water's edge. A stray dog runs on the beach with a large fish in its mouth. It's his lucky day. You've got to seize your luck.

The smugglers' prices are rock bottom – few adventurers dare run the risk. They scatter in every direction with the raging wind.

And the raging wind carries off the prayers of the men kneeling before the sea. They've decided to embark. They wrap up all the way to their heads in black veils, so as not to swallow the sand and the dust. From behind, that child could be him. But when he turns around, I have to accept it's not. Will I ever find Badian again, now that I've lost Augustin?

The sand is grey, the sky is turning black, the sea's in a foul mood. The storm breaks, flurries of sand fly up from the beach and whistle past. Shouldn't I head back to the dusty road that brought me as far as the Atlantic, instead of plunging into the ocean? Or should I try my luck? Like the dog with his fish? Right now, he must be tucking in, sheltered somewhere out of the wind.

Some people are pacing up and down at the water's edge, because they can't make up their minds. Three steps forward, three back. They can't decide. I no longer have a choice. Choice is something that's too expensive for me. Choice is a luxury.

I, Alpha Coulibaly, also known as 'without a dugout', climb into a boat together with Antoine, and Abebi's wrap, but not Augustin.

The sea roars in our ears, the sand whips us. Plenty have stayed on the shore – the ones who changed their minds, the ones who didn't get a place. Even though they'd paid. Darkness shrouds them on the coast. And I can hear their thoughts accompanying us on our way. They're making wishes. Those of us on board owe it to them to stay alive.

The boat's overloaded. But it's still floating. The pilot seems sure of what he's doing. He'll be careful – the person steering us doesn't want to die, as far as I know. I'm sitting at the front of the dugout with Antoine. With the wrap. Without Augustin.

The waves rise up on both sides. They peak and swoop down on the boat. Boom! It's like a punch. Once. The boat pitches. We cling on. The sea is tormenting us. Boom! Twice. The boat's sinking. People throw the ballast overboard. The water containers go first. The boat is sinking. People jump. With ropes.

Those who jumped in are swimming surrounded by water containers. Others are swallowing mouthfuls of water. Some rope themselves together. And then you don't see them any more. Perhaps they didn't know how to swim. Perhaps they've made it back to dry land.

Antoine and I cling to each other, without a sound. No one calls out in the dugout. The pilot manoeuvres his way skilfully. The swell is bad, but the pilot is smart. Some pray. Most are sick. I wet myself. But I don't sense my fear. Antoine remains stoical. Fear has paralysed him. Close your eyes, Antoine. Don't look at who's sitting next to us. Don't say her name.

The wind abates, the waves subside. The wait begins.

I guess the boat is still edging forwards, but I can't feel us moving. It doesn't look as if we're making any progress. We're late because of the storm.

The ocean is a liquid desert dried out by the sun. I can see steam on the surface. There are mirages on the ocean as well, like in the middle of the Sahara. A smooth and liquid desert, like a blazing mirror. The sun beats down on our heads and on our skin.

The Canaries are so close. A few minutes away, as the crow flies. And in good weather. But we're behind schedule, and the hours keep slipping by. I've got a splitting headache. It's as if someone's battering the inside of my skull. A little boy is with a man who isn't his father. Or his uncle either. The boy seems terrorised. I reckon he's being used as currency in some kind of trafficking deal.

Time goes by more slowly on the water. Even more so when you're approaching the end of a forbidden voyage. The final part is the most excruciating. All those pains you ignored until that point jump out at you.

What you're doing is forbidden. You know you might pay for it with your life. Life is weary of what you've inflicted on it, and it wants to abandon you. Life has had enough of you, enough of the water, enough of the sun, enough of the boat.

The closer we get to the Canaries, the more they seem to steal away from us and hide. They're toying with our impatient lives. I've got such a pounding headache. The Canaries are retreating – they're escaping from me.

Darkness falls. The sun has beaten down too hard. The pilot says we have to be cautious, that it's going to take us all night, after all.

A passenger throws herself into the water. Just like that. For no reason. Everybody starts shouting. Some go crazy. Life wants to abandon them. But we owe it to the dead to stay alive. The little boy cries softly.

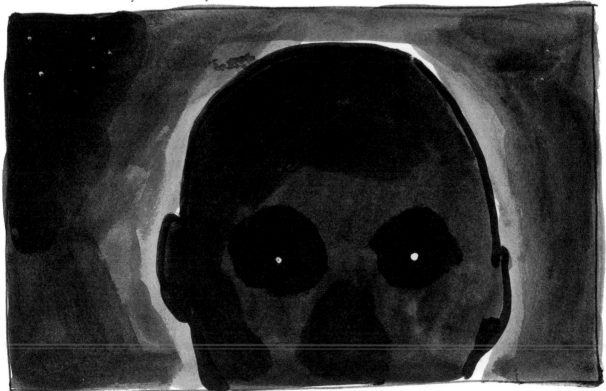

An eight-hour voyage in fair weather, they said. Without incident, without delays, without unforeseen events, without any of life's mishaps. We're going to have to get used to the idea of sleeping here. And perhaps of not waking up. I'd rather not take the risk. I won't sleep.

Sunrise. I thought I saw it ... Land.

It was so close. As if all I needed to do was hold out my hand to touch it. So I gave Abebi's wrap back to the sea. But Antoine says I was hallucinating.

Oh no I wasn't! This time, I'm right. This time, it's for real. This is Spain. Europe. I've made it. Abebi, we've made it.

EPILOGUE

Alpha and Antoine arrived safely in Spain. They were taken care of by a Spanish doctor, who chose to break the law by treating 'illegal' migrants and giving them a roof over their heads.

Among the doctor's patients, Alpha spotted a very sick little boy — Augustin. Augustin had arrived in Spain a few days earlier. After running away from the camp, he had all his money stolen as he tried to return to Gao. He was caught by a child trafficker who sent him to Europe. By a stroke of luck, Augustin fell seriously ill during the crossing. Left for dead on his arrival in Spain, he was taken in by the Spanish doctor.

Alpha stayed by the little boy's side while he got better. Antoine headed off on his own.

Once Augustin had made a full recovery, Alpha took him to France with the intention of contacting the authorities on their arrival. His grandfather's French papers would, he believed, enable him to sort out his own situation, as well as that of Augustin, and of his family, with whom he was confident of being reunited.

In Paris, Alpha did indeed find the Gare du Nord, but nobody knew the whereabouts of his sister-in-law's hair salon. It was winter. For several days, Alpha and Augustin hung around the station, encountering homeless people, until he was directed to a hostel for foreigners. A social worker managed to secure Augustin a school place. But the little boy didn't adapt well. He was determined to find his mother and sister again, and he ran away repeatedly. Each time, they found him at the Gare du Nord, where he thought he could catch a train to Africa. As a minor he wasn't liable to be deported, so the police left him alone.

For his part, Alpha eventually stumbled upon his sister-in-law's salon. She had no news of his wife or son. Alpha acknowledged that they might have died along the way.

Found wandering aimlessly around the Gare du Nord, he was arrested. Detained. Deported.

Alpha is sitting at the back of an aeroplane. He is handcuffed and seated next to another 'illegal' migrant, who jokes that it's taken him eighteen months to reach Europe, and it will take him less than nine hours to return to where he started from.

As for Antoine, he hasn't been spotted playing for Barcelona.

Nobody knows what became of him.

119

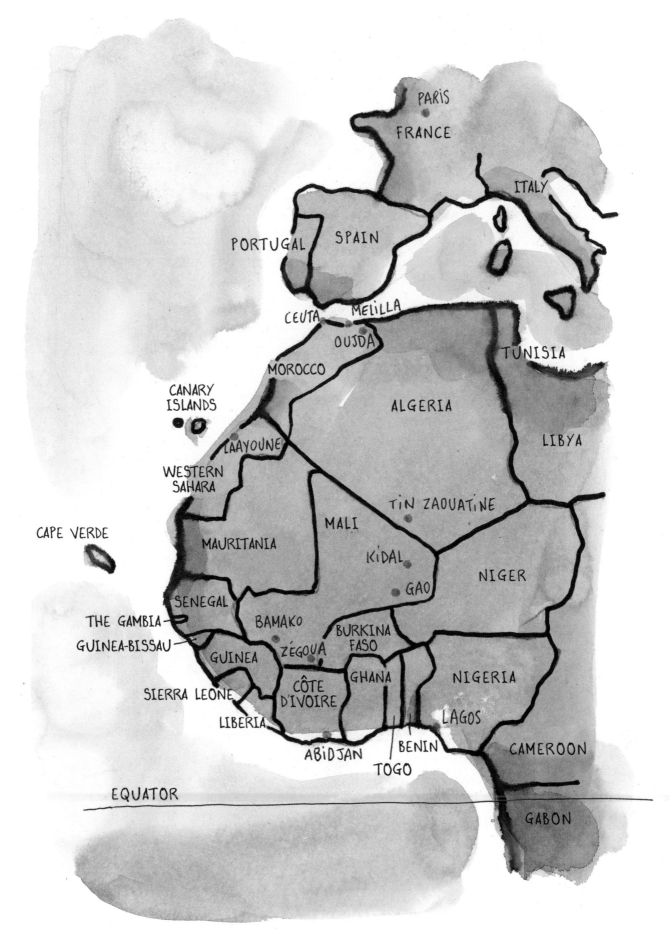

THE ARTIST

BARROUX was born in Paris and spent much of his childhood in North Africa. After studying photography, art, sculpture and architecture, he worked as an art director in Paris and Montreal. While in Montreal, Barroux began creating the traditionally produced images – using linocut, acrylic painting and pencil – that led to his remarkable illustrations for children's books. His previous work includes the glorious *Where's the Elephant*, longlisted for the Kate Greenaway Medal, and *Line of Fire*, based on the diary of an unknown soldier from the First World War. Michael Morpurgo calls *Line of Fire* a "remarkable book".

THE AUTHOR

BESSORA was born in Belgium to a Swiss mother and a Gabonese father, and she grew up in Europe, America and Africa. After a first career in international finance, Bessora was inspired by her travels in South Africa to study anthropology in Paris, where she also wrote her first novel, published in 1999. In 2001 Bessora won the Fénéon Prize for *Les taches d'encre*, and in 2007 her novel *Cueillez-moi jolis messieurs* won the Grand prix littéraire d'Afrique noire. Bessora's writing is free-spirited, demanding and unclassifiable – qualities which she attributes to her varied origins and the many countries she's called home.

THE TRANSLATOR

SARAH ARDIZZONE is an award-winning translator from the French. She has published some 40 titles by writers such as Daniel Pennac, Yasmina Reza and Alexandre Dumas. Sarah has a particular love for translating sharp dialogue, urban and migrant slang and she has twice won the Marsh Award for Children's Literature in Translation. Sarah also curates educational programmes – including Translation Nation, Translators in Schools and the Spectacular Translation Machine – and is a patron of children's world literature charity Outside In World.